JULIUS CAESAR
IN GAUL AND BRITAIN

HISTORY EYEWITNESS

EDITED WITH AN INTRODUCTION
AND ADDITIONAL MATERIAL BY
STEPHEN RIDD

RSVP

RAINTREE STECK-VAUGHN
P U B L I S H E R S
The Steck-Vaughn Company

Austin, Texas

For Barbara

Published by Raintree Steck-Vaughn Publishers, an
imprint of Steck-Vaughn Company

Design by Saffron House, map by Jeff Edwards.

Library of Congress Cataloging-in-Publication Data

Ridd, Stephen.
 Julius Caesar in Gaul and Britain / edited with an introduc-
 tion and additional material by Stephen Ridd.
   p. cm. — (History eyewitness)
 Includes index.
 ISBN 0-8114-8283-9
  1. Caesar, Julius — Military leadership — Juvenile litera-
ture. 2. Vercingetorix, Chief of the Arverni, d. 45? B.C. —
Juvenile literature. 3. Gaul — History — Gallic Wars, 58-51
B.C. — Juvenile literature. 4. Great Britain — History —
Roman period, 55 B.C.-499 A.D. — Juvenile literature.
[1. Caesar, Julius — Military leadership. 2. Gaul — History
— Gallic Wars, 58-51 B.C. 3. Great Britain — History —
Roman period, 55 B.C.-449 A.D.] I. Caesar, Julius. De bello
Gallico. II. Title. III. Series.
DC62.C3R53c 1995
937'.05'092—dc20   94-28699
[B]   CIP AC

Printed in China
Bound in the United States

1 2 3 4 5 6 7 8 9 0 99 98 97 96 95 94

Acknowledgments
The publishers would like to thank the following for
permission to reproduce photographs:

Ancient Art and Architecture Collection: p.11, p.38, p.40, p.42
Ashmolean Museum: p.32
C. M. Dixon: p.8, p.12, p.16, p.18, p.25
e. t. archive: p.30, p.34
The Granger Collection: cover
Louvre, Paris. Photo Réunion des Musée Nationeaux: p.45
ZEFA: p.23, p.29

Every effort has been made to contact copyright holders of material
reproduced in this book. Any omissions will be rectified in
subsequent printings if notice is given to the publisher.

Note to the Reader

In this book some of the words are printed in **bold** type. This indicates that the
word is listed in the glossary on pages 46–47. The glossary gives a brief explana-
tion of words that may be new to you.

CONTENTS

Introduction

Julius Caesar was 55 when he was assassinated on the Ides (fifteenth) of March, 44 B.C. By this time Caesar had risen to a position of supreme power in Rome. He spent nine years of his life, from 58 to 50 B.C. inclusive, campaigning with his army in Gaul. This book gives extracts, in translation, of his account of this Gallic War. Politics and warfare were closely linked in the Roman world, and Caesar was highly talented and highly ambitious in both these fields. In 59 B.C., the year before he first came to Gaul, he had been **consul** in Rome. Two consuls, the most senior public officials in Rome, were elected each year. Their importance was shown by the fact that the Romans reckoned their years by reference to the holders of this office. So events were dated according to which consuls were in power. After their year in office, it was a tradition that they should leave Rome to take command of one of the Roman provinces. Caesar secured for himself a much larger provincial command, which lasted much longer than was normal. His command, in Gaul, northern Italy, and the east Adriatic Coast, lasted for ten years. It gave him enormous opportunities to win glory, riches, and power through the conquest of people who, in the Romans' eyes, were **barbarians.**

The Gaul that Caesar conquered between 58 and 51 B.C. included most of present-day France, but excluded the deep south, which had been a Roman province for over 50 years. It also included southern Holland, Belgium, Germany west of the Rhine, and most of Switzerland. In two famous expeditions, in 55 and 54 B.C., Caesar brought the Roman army to Britain for the first time. The conquest of Britain had to wait another 100 years, until the time of the Emperor Claudius. The cost of the conquest of Gaul in loss of life on the Gallic side was high—the Gauls did not give in to the Romans without a struggle.

The original Latin work *De Bello Gallico* (*About the Gallic War*) is divided into eight books, seven of them by Caesar himself. The last one (not represented here) was written shortly after his death by one of his officers, Aulus Hirtius. Caesar called his own writings "Commentaries," and the name is significant. They are presented not as a highly formal piece of literature but as a simple, unvarnished account of what happened. Almost always Caesar says of himself "Caesar" did this or that, rather than "I" did it, and this helps to give the writing a sense of detachment. Despite this, however, it is clear that Caesar portrays himself throughout in a very favorable light. His aim, in the first place, was to publicize his successes in order to help him in his quest for more power. Beyond this, his work is our only written source of information about the lives and deaths of the Gauls of this time, and the only surviving account written by a great general of the classical world about his own campaigns.

CHAPTER I

Pursue and Destroy

(58 B.C.)

GAUL ON THE EVE OF CAESAR'S ARRIVAL

When Caesar came to Gaul in 58 B.C., it was inhabited by some 200 different tribes. The tribe called the **Helvetii** had been living in what is now Switzerland. Under pressure from their German neighbors, they began moving westward in search of new land. Caesar's command in Gaul gave him the authority to protect the Roman Province in the south from attack. So the mass migration of the Helvetii provided him with a good reason for moving his army deep into territory outside the Roman Province. Three other tribes living to the west of the Helvetii are mentioned in this chapter. They are the Allobroges, the Sequani, and the Aedui. The capital of the last of these was Bibracte (now Mont Beuvray).

The Helvetii got ready to leave their own land. They set fire to all their towns and villages and to any other homes that still remained. They also burned all their wheat, except for what they took with them. They did this so there was no hope of returning home and so they would be more ready to face every kind of danger. Everyone was told to bring three months' supply of wheat, ready ground. The neighboring tribes were persuaded to burn their towns and villages, too, and to set off with them.

There were just two routes that they could take. The first was narrow and difficult, passing between the Jura Mountains and the Rhône River. It just let their wagons through in single file. Dominating this route was a high mountain, so that a handful of men could easily stop them.

The other route took them through the **Province** [today's Provence] and was much easier. The Rhône River is the border between the Helvetii and the Allobroges, a recently pacified tribe. The Allobroges' town closest to Helvetian territory is Geneva, which has a bridge over the river. The Helvetii thought they could either persuade or force the Allobroges to let them pass through their land. So they made everything ready for their departure and set a day on which all were to assemble on the banks of the Rhône. That day was the March 28 in the consulship of Lucius Piso and Aulus Gabinius (58 B.C.).

When Caesar received news of their attempt to pass through the Province, he quickly left Rome and made great haste to reach Gaul. He arrived in the neighborhood of Geneva and ordered the maximum number of soldiers to be raised throughout the Province (there was at this time only one **legion** stationed in Gaul). Then he commanded the destruction of the bridge. When the Helvetii heard of his arrival, they sent **envoys** to him to say that it was their intention to pass through the Province without causing any harm to it, since there was no other route open to them. They were also to say that they asked his permission to do this.

Caesar remembered that on an earlier occasion the Roman army had suffered a humiliating defeat at the hands of the Helvetii, so he did not think that their request should be granted. Nor did he think that enemies like these, if allowed to pass through the Province, would do so peacefully. However, in order to gain time to assemble the troops he had ordered, he told the envoys that he needed a few days to think it over.

Meanwhile he used his legion and the troops that he had assembled in the Province to build a wall and ditch sixteen feet high for nineteen miles, along the bank of the Rhône from the lake of Geneva to the Jura Mountains. This was the border between the lands of the Sequani

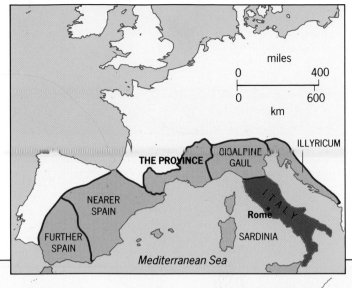

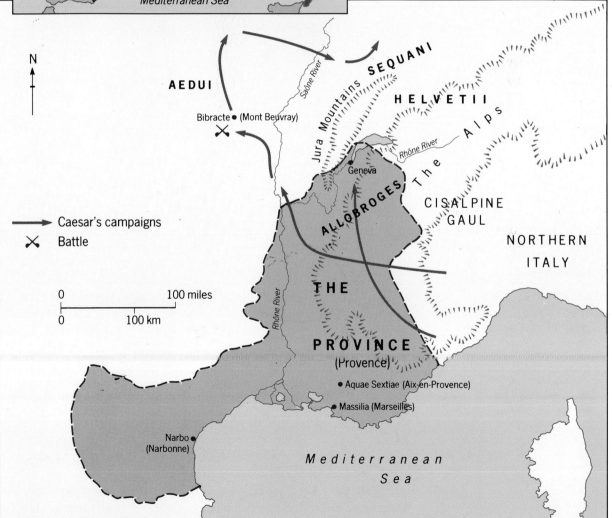

Caesar's campaigns against the Helvetii.

Roman soldiers building a wall. This is one of the relief scenes that decorate Trajan's Column, a column about 100 feet high put up in Rome 150 years after Caesar's time, to commemorate the victories of the Emperor Trajan. It is one of the main sources of visual information about the Roman army.

and the lands of the Helvetii. When this work was finished, he built and manned guard posts all the way along, to make it easier to stop the Helvetii if they tried to cross the border against his wishes. When the day came for the return of the envoys, he said that by a long-established tradition of the Roman state, he could not allow anyone to pass through the Province, and that if they tried to use force, he would stop them. With their hopes dashed in this way, the Helvetii still tried to push across the border. Some joined boats together and made various rafts; others attempted to wade across the river where it was shallowest. Sometimes this took place in broad daylight but more often at night.

Each time they were forced back by the defense works and by attacks from our soldiers, and so they stopped.

Next the Helvetii had in mind to try the other route, through the land of the Sequani and the Aedui. This route was close to the Province. When news of their plan was brought to Caesar, he saw the danger it would mean to the Province to have an enemy of such a warlike character as neighbors in land that was both open and rich in wheat. For these reasons, Caesar left Titus Labienus as overall commander of the defenses and made great haste for Italy. Here he raised two new legions and brought three further legions out of their winter quarters. With these five legions he hurried back to Gaul by the shortest route across the Alps. On the way, certain Alpine tribes seized commanding positions above his army as it passed by and tried to stop them. They were beaten back in a number of battles, and before long Caesar was back in the territory close to the Rhône. By now the Helvetii had led their forces through the narrow pass and across the territory of the Sequani into that of the Aedui, whose fields they were plundering. The Aedui were unable to defend themselves against these attacks and, being long-standing friends of the Roman people, they complained bitterly and asked Caesar to help them. In all the surrounding areas, the story was the same: fields plundered, children taken off into slavery, towns scarcely able to defend themselves from attack, nothing left by the marauders but the bare soil. All of this made Caesar realize that he could not wait while the Helvetii completed their destruction of the property of Rome's allies, as they came ever nearer to the Province.

There is a river called the Saône, which flows through the territory of the Aedui and the Sequani into the Rhône. It is so slow-moving that the eye cannot make out which way it flows. The Helvetii were in the process of crossing this river on rafts and little boats tied together. When his scouts brought news to Caesar that the Helvetii had got three quarters of their forces across the river, and that the remaining quarter were still on the far bank, he set out around midnight with three legions and reached the part of the Helvetian forces that had not yet crossed the river. These he attacked and killed in great number, since they were loaded down with their belongings and were not expecting an attack. The survivors took to their heels and hid in the nearby forests. This group, one of four that together make up the Helvetian people, had left its home once before, within our fathers' lifetime [107 B.C.], and had killed the consul Lucius Cassius and inflicted a humiliating defeat on his army. So, whether by chance or by the design of the immortal gods, that section of the Helvetian people that had brought a catastrophe on the Roman state was the first to suffer for it.

The Roman Army was a highly efficient, well-disciplined force, which spent much of its time on the move. It was equipped to carry out engineering projects, such as the construction of large walls, bridges, and siege works. It completed this work with speed and precision. Keeping this large, mobile force fed required considerable planning and organization. Cereals formed the staple diet in Roman times, and Caesar had to make sure his army was always supplied with wheat.

After this battle was over, Caesar had a bridge built over the Saône in order to pursue the remaining Helvetian forces. The Helvetii were thrown into confusion by his sudden appearance. It had taken them twenty days to cross the river, and even then it had been very difficult. He had done this in a single day. So they sent a delegation to him, led by Divico, who had led the Helvetii in their earlier war against Cassius. He made a speech to Caesar in which he offered terms for a peaceful settlement, but in which he also reminded Caesar of the earlier defeat of the Romans by the Helvetii. He reminded him, too, of the Helvetian people's long tradition of courage in war. The lesson they had learned from their fathers and forefathers before them was this: to rely in war on their courage, rather than on tricks, such as falling on people unawares. Caesar should take care, therefore, unless he wanted the place where they now were to be remembered as the site of a Roman disaster where a whole army fell.

In his reply to this, Caesar said that he was well aware of the matters to which Divico had referred, and that the incident was all the harder to bear, since Rome had done nothing to deserve the attack. But even if he could forget this earlier outrage, how could he overlook their recent behavior? They had attempted to force their way through the Province when he had forbidden it. They had injured the Aedui and other tribes. He added that when the immortal gods wanted to punish people for their crimes, they sometimes had a habit of making those people prosper even more and get away with things even longer, so that when their fortunes changed, they would suffer more acute pain. Even so, if he were granted hostages by them, to show that they were in earnest over what they promised to do, and if they gave compensation to the Aedui and the other tribes for the injuries that they had done them, he could come to a peaceful settlement with them. Divico replied that it was a custom learned by the Helvetii from their forefathers that they should receive, not hand over, hostages, and with these words he left.

Next day the Helvetii moved camp. So, too, did Caesar, and he sent forward all his cavalry, about 4,000, to see in which direction the enemy were moving. This cavalry force attacked the rear of the Helvetian column too enthusiastically. They fought the Helvetian cavalry on unfavorable ground. A few of our men fell. The Helvetii were delighted to think that 500 of their cavalry had driven back a much larger cavalry force of ours. From time to time, they made a stand with increasing boldness, and their rear guard mounted attacks on our men. Caesar held his men back from battle and was content for the moment to restrain the enemy from foraging, plundering, and looting. So the two armies continued on their way for about a fortnight (two weeks), with no more than five or six miles separating the end of one from the front of the other.

When the time for giving out the wheat ration to the troops was only two days off, Caesar turned his attention to this process and diverted his army from its pursuit of the Helvetii in order to make for the nearest town, Bibracte. This was by far the greatest and richest town of the Aedui and was no more than eighteen miles away. News of this change was brought to the enemy by runaway slaves, and they, too, changed direction and began to make attacks on our rear. Seeing this, Caesar drew his forces aside onto a neighboring hill. Halfway up the hill he put his four veteran legions in three lines of battle. At the top of the hill, he stationed the two legions recently raised in Italy and all the **auxiliary forces.** Meanwhile he gave orders for all the baggage to be collected and for defenses to be dug to protect it, by those posted high up on the hill.

The Helvetii followed with all their wagons, collected their belongings together, and formed up into as tight a line as they could. They fought off an attack made by our cavalry and advanced toward our front line in phalanx formation. Caesar spoke words of encouragement to his men and joined battle. The soldiers threw their spears from the higher ground and easily broke the enemy phalanx; then they drew their swords and charged.

The Roman spears caused the Helvetii considerable problems as one often went through more than one of their shields and fastened them together. The soft iron head was made to bend on impact, and they could neither pull it out nor fight properly with their left hands

Part of a marble relief from a Roman altar of about 100 B.C., showing Roman legionary soldiers. The legions formed the backbone of Caesar's army and were all infantry soldiers. Each legion contained about 5,000 men, and the number of legions Caesar had in Gaul varied between six and eleven. Caesar inspired great devotion, and his favorite legion, which often comes into these stories, was the tenth.

hampered in this way. Many tried for some time to shake their shields free, but finally gave up and chose to throw the shields away and fight with their bodies unprotected. In the end they were worn out by their wounds and began to retreat to a hill about a mile away. But as our men advanced on them, some 15,000 allies of the Helvetii, who had been protecting the rear of their column, came straight into action and launched an attack on our exposed right flank. Seeing this, the Helvetii, who had retreated to the hill, surged forward again and began to renew the fight.

The battle was now raging on two fronts, and the fighting was long and hard. When they could not withstand our attacks any longer, the Helvetii withdrew as before to the hill. Their allies gathered round the wagons and the baggage and continued to put up a resistance until they were captured by our forces. Throughout this whole battle, which lasted from midday till evening, not one single enemy was seen running away.

The survivors on the Helvetian side, numbering about 130,000, marched through the night. Three days were allowed to our soldiers for tending the wounded and burying the dead, but Caesar sent a message to the neighboring tribe forbidding them to offer the Helvetii food or other assistance. Then when the three days were over, he set off in pursuit of the Helvetii with all his forces.

Driven by a complete lack of resources, the Helvetii sent envoys to Caesar to surrender. He demanded that they should give him hostages, hand over their arms, and return the runaway slaves. The Helvetii and their allies were then ordered to return to their own land. Since they had no food at home to avoid the threat of starvation, Caesar told the Allobroges to supply them with food. He then ordered the Helvetii to rebuild the towns and villages that they had burned.

In the camp of the Helvetii were discovered certain records written on wax tablets using the Greek alphabet. These were taken to Caesar. They showed the numbers of those who had left their homes. Figures were given for those who could bear arms, for the children, the old men, and the women. The grand total was 368,000, and of these the Helvetii themselves made up 263,000. The number of those who could bear arms was 92,000. On Caesar's orders, a census was taken of those who returned home, and the number was found to be 110,000.

If these chilling statistics can be trusted, they show that over a quarter of a million people, many of them women and children, were killed during this campaign. The Romans back home would be delighted to hear of Caesar's success in achieving such a large-scale slaughter of barbarian forces, and those Gauls threatened by the mass migration of the Helvetii would also have cause to feel grateful to Caesar.

In another scene from Trajan's Column, Roman soldiers bring a barbarian prisoner to their commander.

13

CHAPTER 2

A Hard-Won Victory

(57 B.C.)

THE SPREADING POWER OF ROME

Roman merchants generally found a ready market for their products among the Gauls, especially for Italian wine. The vine was not grown at this time in Gaul and imported Italian wine was sold for high prices. In 57 B.C. Caesar campaigned against the warlike Belgic tribes, who lived in the north of Gaul, beyond the Seine River. This shows that he intended to conquer areas far beyond those he conquered in the previous year. Besides his legionary soldiers, he had with him a number of auxiliary forces. These included several thousand cavalry, who came from Gaul and later from Germany.

Caesar made inquiries about the character and customs of the Nervii (a tribe living in present-day Belgium) and learned the following information: merchants were not allowed into their country, and the importing of wine and other luxury goods was banned. They believed that these things made men lose their ability to be brave warriors. He learned, too, that the Nervii were a fierce people, of outstanding bravery, who criticized the other Belgae for giving in to the Romans and failing to live up to the bravery of their ancestors. They made it clear that they would never send envoys or accept peace on any terms.

When he had marched for three days through their territory, Caesar began to hear, from prisoners, of a river called the Sambre, some ten miles beyond his present camp. On the far side of that river, all the Nervii had taken up position and were waiting with the neighboring tribes for the Romans to arrive. Reinforcements were on their way to join them. The women and those who were either too young or too old to fight had been placed for safety in an area of marshes, which was impossible for an army to reach.

When he had found all this out, he sent forward his scouts and **centurions** to choose a suitable place for a camp. Many of the Belgae had surrendered by now, and these and other Gallic tribesmen had joined Caesar and were marching with him. A party of these, as it was later discovered from prisoners, had made a note of the order in which our army regularly marched during those days, and came by night to the Nervii with this information, urging them to attack the first legion when it reached camp well ahead of the others, and while the soldiers were still loaded down with their packs. There was another thing that helped in this plan. The Nervii never made use of cavalry, preferring to rely in war on their infantry. But to make it easier to stop raids from their neighbors mounted on horseback, they had made a system of hedges, not unlike a wall, that could neither be penetrated nor even seen through. Since these hindered our army's progress, the Nervii thought that the opportunity was too good to miss.

The site chosen by our men for the camp was a piece of land sloping gently down to the Sambre River. On the far side of the river, the ground sloped upward with the same gradient, so as to form a second hill exactly opposite the first. For about two hundred yards at the foot of this second hill, the ground was open, but higher up; it was wooded and hard to see into. The enemy forces remained out of sight in these woods. On the open ground along the river bank, a few groups of cavalry were visible. The river was about three feet deep.

Caesar had sent his cavalry on ahead and was following close behind with all his forces, but the order in which they were marching was not that which the Belgae had described to the Nervii. Caesar was

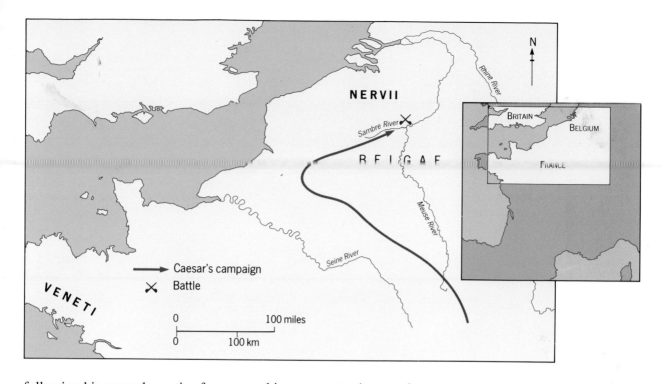

Caesar's campaign against the Nervii.

following his normal practice for approaching enemy territory and was at the head of six legions that were ready for combat. Behind them he had stationed the baggage and equipment for the whole army, then came the two legions which had most recently been raised, at the rear of the column. Their task was to protect the baggage.

Our cavalrymen, together with the slingers and archers, crossed the river and joined battle with the enemy cavalry. The enemy's tactics were to keep falling back to their own lines inside the woods and then to re-emerge from the woods and make repeated charges on our men. Our soldiers pursued them only as far as the open ground allowed. In the meantime, the six legions that had been the first to arrive measured out the site and began work constructing the camp. The moment when the forces hidden in the woods got their first glimpse of our baggage and equipment was the time they had fixed on among themselves to launch their attack. The battle-line had been drawn up and the men were already armed inside the wood. They urged each other on and suddenly came bursting out of the wood all at once, aiming for our cavalrymen. These were easily routed and thrown into confusion. Then, with incredible speed, the enemy forces charged down to the river. They seemed at almost the same moment to be beside the wood, in the river and at close range. With the same speed they charged uphill towards our camp and those working there.

Caesar had everything to do at once: the red flag had to be hoisted up as a signal for an immediate call to arms, the trumpet signal given, the soldiers recalled from their work, the parties that had gone off in search of building material for the earthworks had to be brought back, the battle line drawn up, the troops spurred on, and the signal for action given. The speed of the enemy's approach gave him hardly a moment to do all this. Two things, however, helped to save the situation: the soldiers were well drilled, and they had already been in battle. From their experience they knew what they had to do without being told, and their **officers** had been told by Caesar not to leave their legions and the work they were engaged in until the camp was finished. Because the enemy were now so close and their attack had been so fast, these officers did not wait for orders from Caesar but took the initiative themselves.

After giving the necessary orders, Caesar ran down to spur on any soldiers he chanced to find and came upon the tenth legion. He only had time to tell them to retain the memory of their former courage and not to panic, but to resist the enemy attack bravely. The enemy were within range of the Romans' spears, and so he gave the signal to join battle. Setting off in another direction to spur on more of his men, he found them already in the thick of the fighting. Time was so short and the enemy so set on battle that there was not a moment to put on helmets or take the covers off shields, let alone fix on divisional colors. The men left their work and took their stand wherever they chanced to find themselves, wherever they first saw the **standards.** There was no time to waste looking for their comrades in action.

The way the army was drawn up was dictated more by the sloping nature of the land and by the needs of the moment than by any consideration of tactics. The legions were separated from each other and were resisting the enemy in different parts of the battlefield. Dense hedges, as we explained earlier, obscured the view, so that reinforcements could not be brought into position. It was impossible to see what was going to be needed in any one place and impossible for one man to give all the orders. The situation was confused, and the fortunes of the troops varied accordingly.

Soldiers of the ninth and tenth legions, stationed on the left of the battle line, threw their javelins, and since the enemy were exhausted from their charge and had suffered heavy casualties, they were easily driven from the higher ground into the river. There they got into difficulties trying to cross, and our men ran after them and killed great numbers of them with their swords. Nor did our men hesitate to cross the river and advance up the rising ground. The enemy resisted them again, and the battle started once more, but our men put them to

THE STRUCTURE OF COMMAND IN THE ROMAN ARMY

Below Caesar, the army's commander-in-chief, were a number of subordinate officers, appointed by him. He would give them duties such as taking command of a legion in a battle, obtaining supplies, or superintending the building of ships. The most important of Caesar's officers was called Titus Labienus. Each legion had six **military tribunes.** These were young men of well-to-do families, gaining experience as army officers, before going on to a career in public office. The centurions were the most experienced soldiers and were promoted from the ranks for their bravery. Each legion had 60 centurions, arranged in order of seniority, each with command of some 80–100 men. Once the soldiers were in camp, a red flag was hoisted as a signal for moving camp or for battle.

In this scene (left) *from Trajan's Column, Roman soldiers are shown busily constructing a camp. These camps followed a regular pattern: they were square, and the area marked out was first surrounded by a defensive ditch. Inside the square, a mound of earth was piled up as the ditch was dug out. On the top of the mound a palisade (fence) of stakes was fixed. Aerial photography can still sometimes show the outlines of Roman camps.*

flight. Similarly in another part of the battlefield, two separate legions, the eleventh and the eighth, drove the enemy down from the higher ground onto the very banks of the river. However, this meant that virtually the whole front and left of the camp were left exposed.

All the Nervii under their supreme commander, Boduognatus, made a massed attack on this part of it. Some of his men began to outflank the two legions, the twelfth and the seventh, who at some distance from each other were defending the right of the camp, while others made for the high ground where the camp was sited.

At the same time, the cavalry together with the light-armed infantry, whom I mentioned as being put to flight by the first enemy attack, made their way back to camp, only to meet the enemy forces there. They ran for their lives once more, in a different direction. The camp servants, who had watched from the back gate at the top of the hill and seen our men advance victoriously and cross the river, came out in

*Roman forces are shown in action against barbarians in a scene from a Roman **sarcophagus**. The barbarians fight naked, protected only by their shields and by the **torcs**, which they believed to be magic, around their necks.*

search of **booty**. But when they looked back and saw the enemy moving about inside our camp, they, too, ran away at top speed. Also at this time a noise of confused shouting arose from those who were coming with the baggage and equipment and who were now panic-stricken and were running away in all directions. Some Gallic cavalrymen had been sent to Caesar from their homeland as auxiliary forces (these were a tribe known as the Treveri and had a high reputation among the Gauls for their bravery). They saw the desperate state of affairs and hurried home with the news that the Romans had been routed and beaten, and that the enemy had taken the Roman camp with all its equipment.

Caesar saw how hard-pressed his men were and how impossible it was to bring reinforcements in to their aid. He snatched a shield from one of the soldiers who was well back from the front line (as the commanding officer, he did not normally carry a shield), and made his way to the front line. Here he called aloud on the centurions, each by name, and urged the others on to greater efforts. He gave orders to advance and to spread out, to make it easier for the men to use their swords. His arrival gave the soldiers new hope and strengthened their resolve. Each man wanted to be seen by his commander to be doing his best, even at the risk of his own life, and so the enemy attack was for a time halted.

Seeing that the seventh legion, stationed close by, was under equally heavy attack from the enemy, Caesar told the military tribunes to bring the two legions gradually together, then to wheel round to face the enemy. This done, the soldiers were able to give each other help and were not afraid of being surrounded and attacked from behind. This made them resist more boldly and fight more bravely. Meanwhile the soldiers of the two legions that had been at the rear of the marching column, guarding the baggage and equipment, got word of the battle

CAESAR'S "MERCY"

Caesar liked to be seen as merciful to those he had conquered, but he applied this mercy as, and when, it suited him. The Belgic tribes were given a demonstration of Roman strength in the campaign against the Nervii, but other, more cooperative tribes were shown the benefits of friendship and support from the Romans.

19

and hurried to the top of the hill, where they were seen by the enemy. Titus Labienus, too, who had captured the enemy camp and could see from his vantage-point on higher ground what was going on in our camp, sent the tenth legion to the rescue of our forces. They heard of the critical state of affairs from the fleeing cavalry and camp servants, and they came as fast as they could.

Their arrival on the scene brought about such a change that even those men who had been wounded and had fallen to the ground leaned on their shields and renewed the fight. Then the camp servants, seeing the enemy were panic-stricken, went out against them, the unarmed against the armed. The cavalry, too, were keen to wipe out the disgrace of their flight by acts of bravery and fought in every place where they could demonstrate their superiority to the legionary soldiers. As for the enemy, even as their hopes of survival were fading, they displayed such courage that when their front ranks fell, those immediately behind stood on top of them and fought on over their bodies. Then when they, too, had been struck down and the corpses had been piled high, the survivors were left, as it were, on a sort of hill, still hurling their spears at our men and still catching our javelins and sending them back. So it ought not to be thought a rash gamble that men of such bravery should have dared to cross a river of such great breadth, climbed banks that were so steep, and advanced over ground that was so greatly to their disadvantage. The most difficult tasks were made easy by their bravery.

After this battle was over, the people and the very name of the Nervii were all but wiped out. The old men, who, as we said, had been gathered together with the children and women and placed among the marshes, were told about the battle. They could see no hope of obstructing the victors and no hope of safety for the vanquished, and so it was universally agreed among the survivors that they should send a **delegation** to Caesar and surrender. In recounting the calamity that had befallen their state, they said that their ruling council had been reduced from 600 to 3 and their fighting men from 60,000 to barely 500. Caesar wanted it to be seen that he was generous toward unfortunate people who begged for mercy, and so he took great care over their safety, ordering that they should retain their territory and towns intact and forbidding their neighbors to attack them.

Caesar thought that Gaul was quiet, and he had left the area when war suddenly broke out. The cause of this war was as follows. The young Publius Crassus was in winter quarters with the seventh legion, close to the Atlantic coast. Since wheat was in short supply in this area, he had sent out officers and military tribunes to the neighboring tribes in search of wheat. Two of these, Quintus Velanius and Titus Silius, were sent to the Veneti.

The Veneti are a people who dominate the whole coastal region in this area. Partly this is because they have more ships than anyone else and regularly use these to sail to Britain, and partly because they are better than the others in their knowledge and practice of seafaring. The coastline here is exposed to the full fury of the sea, with only a few scattered harbors, all of which are in the possession of the Veneti, so virtually everyone who uses the sea has to pay the Veneti for the privilege of doing so. This tribe opened hostilities by holding Silius and Velanius prisoner. They thought that by doing so they would get back the hostages they had given to Crassus. Their influence in the region was enough to prompt their neighbors to do likewise (the Gauls are a hasty and unpredictable people), and two more Roman officers were detained.

Messengers were quickly sent around to the tribal chieftains, and an oath was sworn that they would all act together and would all share the same fate, however things turned out. They also put pressure on the other tribes to choose the freedom that they had inherited from their forefathers rather than slavery to the Romans. The whole Atlantic coast was soon won over to their way of thinking and a joint delegation was sent to Publius Crassus: if he wanted his men back, he must first return the hostages.

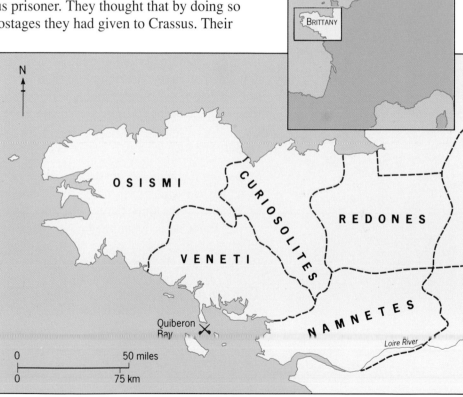

Caesar's campaign against the Veneti.

Crassus sent news of these developments to Caesar, who, being too far away to deal with them himself, gave orders in the meantime for warships to be built on the Loire River, which flows out into the Atlantic, for rowers to be assembled from the Province, and for sailors and helmsmen to be made ready. Having personally seen to all these matters, Caesar hurried to join his army as soon as the time of year permitted him.

The Veneti and the other tribes learned of Caesar's arrival and realized the full significance of the crime they had committed. They had detained an official delegation and thrown them into prison, when all nations of the world have always insisted on giving safe passage to such people. Considering the great danger that they were now in, they began preparations for war, concentrating on making their ships ready for action. They trusted in the natural advantages of their region, and this gave them greater confidence. They knew that tidal estuaries stopped attacks over land, while attack by sea was made hazardous by our lack of knowledge of the coast and by the scarcity of harbors. They were also sure that a lack of wheat meant that our armies could not stay much longer in the area. Even if they were attacked, they depended on the great strength of their fleet. The Romans had no knowledge of the **shoals,** the harbors, or the islands in the area where they were planning to fight. It was one thing, in their view, to sail in the enclosed waters of the Mediterranean, but quite another thing to venture out into the vast, open seas of the Atlantic Ocean.

So having made these calculations, they fortified their strongholds, brought their wheat in from the fields, and assembled on the coast of Venetia all the ships they could find, for they thought that it was certain that Caesar would begin his attack here. A considerable number of other tribes joined them, and they sent for help from Britain, which lies opposite this region of Gaul.

This was not a good place to fight a war. Nevertheless, for a number of reasons, Caesar felt he must fight. There was the crime of holding Roman envoys prisoner, the rebellion, and outbreak of hostilities after a formal surrender and the handing over of hostages. Also the uprising had spread to so many tribes, and above all, there was the fear that if this region were allowed to go unpunished, people in all the other districts would think they could get away with it, too. So realizing that virtually the whole of Gaul was in the mood for rebellion and was being whipped up for war, and that people everywhere want their freedom and hate slavery, he decided that he should split his army up and distribute it over a wider area, before any other states had time to join the uprising. Officers with their contingents were given specific orders and sent off in different directions. He put the young Decius

Brutus in charge of the fleet and the Gallic ships that he had ordered from those regions that had already been pacified, telling him to make the earliest possible start for the territory of the Veneti. He himself hurried in the same direction at the head of the land forces.

The strongholds of the Veneti were generally situated on the tips of headlands jutting out into the sea. This made it hard to attack them by land, since every twelve hours the tide came pounding in from the sea and cut them off. Nor could ships be used, since at low tide, they would run aground and be damaged in the shallows. Thus either means of attacking their strongholds had its problems. Also, even if building operations on a colossal scale proved a threat to them, by walling off the incoming tide and creating access on a level with their town walls, they could simply abandon the defense of one stronghold, bring in vast numbers of ships, of which they had a never-ending supply, extract all their possessions, and then retire to the next stronghold, where they would have the same natural advantages in starting their defense again. This policy they put into operation for most of the summer, and it was easy for them, since our ships were held up by storms and by the almost insuperable difficulties of sailing in the vast, open seas where the tides ran high and where there was no more than a scattering of harbors.

The ships of the Veneti were built and equipped in the following manner. Their hulls were considerably flatter than those of our ships, and this helped them in shallow water and at low tide. Their bows and sterns stood high up out of the water and were designed to stand buffeting from great waves and storms at sea. The ships were built entirely from oak, so as to withstand all kinds of strain and rough handling. The cross timbers were made of beams a foot wide, held together with iron bolts as thick as a man's thumb. Their anchors were held fast with iron chains instead of ropes, and instead of canvas sails, they used animal skins and leather, beaten thin. This may have been because the Veneti had no **flax** and no knowledge of its use, or as seems more likely, because they thought that ordinary sails could not stand up to the gales of Atlantic storms and could not adequately guide such heavy ships.

THE ROMAN NAVY

The Romans had comparatively little experience of naval warfare. At first, the light Roman warships built by Labienus on the Loire River were no match for the heavy oak barges of the Veneti. In the sea battle in Quiberon Bay, Roman ingenuity found a way of putting the enemy ships out of action. The Romans were lucky that the remainder were becalmed at the crucial moment, and so became sitting ducks.

Promontories in the Quiberon Bay district of the southern Brittany coast. The Veneti lived on rocky headlands like these, and the sea battle between the Romans and the Veneti was fought in these waters.

In challenging these ships our fleet had only one advantage—superior speed given by their rowers. In all other respects, in their adaptation to the region and to the violence of its storms, the enemy's ships had the advantage. In addition, our ships could not use their ramming skill to inflict damage, since the enemy ships were too firmly built for this to work, nor could our weapons easily reach up to their superior height. For the same reason, **grappling irons** were of little effect against them. Finally, when a gale began to rage and the ships were allowed to run before the wind, theirs could more easily endure the storms than ours, and once they had left the high seas could rest more safely at anchor in the shallows, with no fear of damage from underwater rocks and shoals. Every one of these things, on the other hand, was a cause of anxiety for our ships.

Caesar took by storm several of the enemy strongholds, before he realized that all these efforts were useless, that he could neither put a stop to their flight by capturing their strongholds nor inflict any damage on them. He decided to wait, therefore, for the arrival of his fleet. The moment the fleet had assembled and had been seen by the enemy, some 220 of their ships, all ready for action and equipped in all kinds of different ways, set out from port and took up position opposite our ships.

Neither Brutus, who was in overall command of the fleet, nor the military tribunes and centurions, who had responsibility for the individual ships, had a clear idea of what they ought to do or what tactics they ought to employ, for they knew that they could not damage the enemy by ramming them. Even when our ships had turrets built on them, they still did not reach the height of the enemy's sterns and were too low for the weapons to reach their target properly, while those hurled by the Gauls fell with greater impact. One device prepared by our troops was of great use to them, and that was specially sharpened hooks, fixed tightly on the end of long poles. With these they got a grip on the ropes that tied the **yardarms** to the masts, pulled them taut, and then snapped them by rowing their own ships vigorously in the opposite direction. When these ropes were cut, there was nothing to stop the yardarms from falling down, and since the Gauls' ships relied entirely on their sails and rigging, once these were lost, the ships were instantly rendered useless. From then on, the struggle was a matter of bravery in combat, something in which our soldiers easily had the upper hand, the more so since the whole action took place under the eyes of Caesar and of the whole army, so that no display of bravery, however small, went unnoticed. Every hill and every patch of high ground that gave a view at close range out over the sea was filled by the army.

When the yardarms had been brought down in the manner described, two or three of our ships would surround the enemy's ships one at a time, and our **marines** would use every ounce of energy to board them. When several of their ships had been stormed and taken, the barbarians realized what was happening, and finding no way to remedy the situation, they quickly began to flee for safety. Turning their ships to have the wind behind them, they suddenly found that the wind had dropped and that there was an absolute calm, making it impossible for them to move. This was just what was needed to end the battle. Our men went after the enemy ships one by one, stormed them all, and captured them, so that by nightfall only a handful of the original number reached land. The battle had lasted from about ten o'clock in the morning till sunset.

This battle brought to an end the war against the Veneti and the whole Atlantic coastal region. All their fighting men had been enlisted including those older men who had some reputation for good judgment or some standing in their community. All the ships that they could muster had been brought into one place. Now that these had gone, the survivors had no means of retreat and no means of defending their strongholds, and so they gave themselves up, with all their possessions, to Caesar. The punishment that Caesar decreed for them was an unusually harsh one, in order to make the Gauls more careful in the future about respecting the rights of envoys. All their leaders were put to death, and the rest of the population were sold off as slaves.

Relief of a Roman warship. The ship's prow tapers into a sharp point for ramming the enemy. At the stern, one of the helmsman's two large steering paddles can be seen.

CHAPTER 4

First Time Over the Channel

(55 B.C.)

The summer was almost over, and although winter starts early in these parts, Caesar was keen to set out for Britain. He was well aware that throughout almost all his campaigns in Gaul the Britons had given help to our enemies. Even if the lateness of the season ruled out a fresh campaign, he still thought it would be very useful for him at least to see the island and its inhabitants. He wanted to know what it was like, where the harbors were, and how it could be approached. All this was virtually unknown in Gaul, for only merchants were hardy enough to make the crossing, and the extent of their knowledge was limited to the coastal areas opposite Gaul. Even though he summoned merchants from every quarter, he was unable to get any information. No one knew the size of the island, the extent to which it was inhabited, the methods of war and other customs of its inhabitants, or the location of harbors suitable for a fleet of large ships.

Before putting himself and his men at risk, he decided that Gaius Volusenus was the man to find all these things out for him and sent him off in a warship, with orders to make a thorough investigation and to come back as soon as he could. He himself set off with all his forces into the territory of the Morini, for it was from there that the shortest crossing to Britain could be made. He ordered ships to assemble here from all the surrounding areas, including the fleet that he had constructed the previous summer for the war against the Veneti. Meanwhile news of his plans was brought by merchants to Britain. Envoys came to him from several of the island's tribes, promising to hand over hostages and to accept Roman rule. These were given generous promises in return and were urged to keep to their decision. On their return home, a special envoy went with them. His name was Commius, and he had been installed by Caesar as king of the Atrebates. He was considered to be a loyal friend and was a man with far-reaching authority in the area. Caesar gave him instructions to go to as many tribes as he could and urge them to declare loyalty to the Romans, adding that he himself would soon be coming there. When Volusenus had seen as much of the territory as he could, without actually disembarking and running the risk of an encounter with the barbarians, he returned to bring his report to Caesar. He had been away four days.

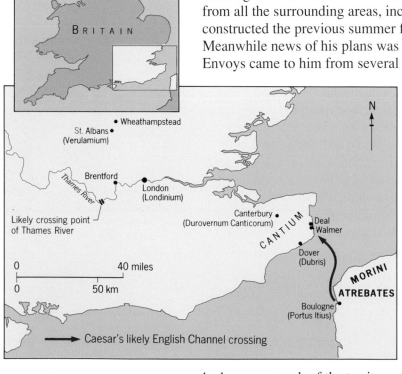

Caesar's first expedition to Britain

Caesar demanded a large number of hostages from the Morini to secure their loyalty. Then he ordered about 80 transport ships to be assembled (enough to transport two legions), and he divided what warships he had among his **quaestor**, his subordinate officers, and the commanders of the auxiliary forces. A further eighteen transport ships were held up by the wind eight miles away and were unable to reach the same harbor as the others. These were assigned to the cavalry. Careful arrangements were made for those staying behind. Then after waiting for good weather conditions for a crossing, he set out around midnight. The cavalry were told to make their way to the further harbor, get on board the transport ships, and follow him. These arrangements, however, took rather longer than he had hoped.

Around nine o'clock in the morning, Caesar reached Britain with his first ships. There, stretched out along the cliffs, they saw lines of enemy troops, heavily armed. The coastline here was made up of cliffs with only a narrow beach between them and the sea. Consequently, the enemy could rain their missiles down from the cliff tops. Realizing that this was not the place to land, he waited at anchor till mid-afternoon for the other ships to arrive. In the meantime, he summoned his officers and military tribunes to tell them what he had learned from Volusenus and to set out his plans. Then when the wind and the tide were right, he gave the sign, weighed anchor, and sailed on for some seven miles, before bringing his ships aground on an open, gently shelving beach.

The Britons, however, had realized what the Romans had in mind and had sent their cavalry and charioteers on ahead. (Chariots are equipment they make great use of in their battles.) While the rest of their forces followed, they stopped our men from making their landing. This landing was a matter of extreme difficulty. Because of their size, the ships could only stand in deep water, and this meant that the soldiers had to jump down from the ships, find their balance amid the waves, and fight with the enemy all at the same moment. Our men did not know the ground, had their hands full, and were weighed down with heavy weapons, while the enemy stood on dry land or took a few steps out into the water, had nothing to encumber their limbs, and knew every inch of the ground. They could launch bold volleys of missiles and come galloping up on horses that were trained for this kind of fighting. All of these things spread panic among our men. They were used to battles on land, not to this new kind of fighting, and as a result, they did not display their usual alacrity and eagerness.

Realizing these problems, Caesar ordered his warships to be rowed round quickly to take up position a little way from the transport ships

CAESAR'S FIRST EXPEDITION TO BRITAIN

In crossing the Channel with his army in the late summer of 55 B.C., Caesar was venturing beyond the boundary of the known world of his day. This adventure was bound to add to his fame, especially as Britain was fabled to be rich in gold, silver, and pearls. However, this first expedition to Britain lasted only about three weeks, and nearly ended in disaster. The officer who was given the task of making a preliminary reconnaissance was Gaius Volusenus, a military tribune of whom Caesar thought highly. The Gallic king, Commius, was also sent to Britain to prepare the way for the Romans. This man was a "client king", the ruler of a local tribe (the Atrebates), who was supported by the Romans in return for his collaboration with them. The expeditionary force, of some 10,000 infantry together with supporting personnel, probably set sail from Portus Itius (Boulogne). The officer known as a "quaestor," was primarily in charge of financial affairs, but here is in command of a warship.

Each Roman legion had a silver eagle, mounted on top of a long pole and carried into battle by the eagle-bearer. It acted as a focus for the legion's sense of identity and loyalty. The loss of this eagle was a matter of supreme disgrace to the legion. Besides the legionary eagle, there were other "standards" that marked the various divisions within the legion. These served as rallying points and were important if the army were to maintain its formation in battle.

on the open, undefended side of the enemy. Then he told the slingers, archers, and catapult operators to open fire. This helped our men, for the barbarians were alarmed by the unfamiliar appearance of the warships, by the movement of the oars, and by the catapults, which they had never seen before. They halted and even retreated a little. At this moment, while our men were still hesitating, mostly because of the depth of the water, the eagle-bearer of the tenth legion called aloud on the gods to grant that his example might bring the legion good fortune, and said, "Jump into the water, comrades, unless you want to surrender our eagle to the enemy. I, at least, shall do my duty for my country and my commander." Then he threw himself overboard and started to carry the eagle toward the enemy. Our soldiers told each other that they could not allow the disgrace of losing the eagle, and to a man, they all leaped overboard. When those on the nearby ships saw this, they followed their example and closed in on the enemy.

Both sides fought hard. Our men were in a lot of trouble. They could not keep their ranks, or get a firm footing, or follow their own standards. They grouped around whatever standards they could find, as they landed from the various ships. The enemy, on the other hand, knew all the shallows and watched from the shore to see when the soldiers were clambering overboard. Then they would gallop up in superior numbers and attack our men in ones and twos, when they could not use their hands to resist. Meanwhile, others standing on our open, exposed side threw their weapons at the whole incoming army.

When Caesar realized what was happening, he gave orders for little boats filled with soldiers to put out from the warships. Wherever he saw that his troops were in difficulties, these boats were sent to help them. The moment our men were on dry land, they all managed to regroup with their comrades. They charged the enemy and put them to flight. They could not follow them very far, however, since the cavalry had been unable to reach the island and had had to turn back. This was the one thing missing, the one thing that would have given Caesar his usual success.

Defeated in battle, the enemy fled, and when they stopped running, they at once sent envoys to make peace with Caesar. They promised to hand over hostages and to do whatever he ordered. With these envoys came Commius, king of the Atrebates, whom I mentioned earlier. The Britons had arrested him and thrown him in chains when he landed and started acting as Caesar's mouthpiece, giving them all kinds of orders in Caesar's name. After the battle they sent him back. They begged Caesar's forgiveness, blaming the common people for what had happened and asking him to excuse them for their ignorance. Caesar complained of the way they had attacked him without any

provocation, especially when they had first sent envoys to him on the European Continent to make peace, but said that he forgave them for their ignorance, and demanded hostages.

A few nights later there was a full moon, and although our men did not know this, the time of the full moon regularly marked the climax of the Atlantic storms. In one short space of time, the warships beached on the shore were filled with sea water, and the transport ships, lying at anchor, were buffeted by the storm. Our men had no chance of responding to this emergency and helping to keep the ships safe. Several of the ships were broken up, and the others, having lost their cables and anchors and all the rest of their tackle, were

The White Cliffs of Dover, stretching away to the right of the picture toward the sandy beach, somewhere near Deal and Walmer, where Caesar landed.

unseaworthy. This sent the whole army into a state of alarm. There were no other ships for the return journey and nothing of any use for repairing the ships. As everyone thought that they would be back in Gaul for the winter, no arrangements had been made to ensure a wheat supply to last the winter in Britain.

When the British chiefs who had assembled before Caesar after the battle got to hear of this, they met together to make plans. They could see that the Romans had no cavalry, no ships, and no wheat supply, and they could tell from the small size of the camp that there were not many soldiers either. It seemed an ideal opportunity for mounting a rebellion, blocking our men off from their wheat and provisions and drawing things out until the winter set in. If only, they thought, they could defeat this force, or make sure that it never returned home, then no one else would ever again try to cross the English Channel to invade their homeland.

Considering the disaster to his ships and the fact that the Britons had stopped sending hostages, Caesar had his suspicions that something like this would happen. So each day he had wheat brought into camp from the fields, and he used wood and bronze from the most severely damaged ships to repair the others. Meanwhile additional material for

Roman soldiers reaping wheat, in a scene from Trajan's Column.

repairs was ordered from the Continent. The soldiers put all their energies into repairing the ships, and in the end they made all but twelve seaworthy.

On one occasion during this period, the seventh legion was out on a routine mission, collecting wheat. Nothing as yet had happened to arouse suspicions of a renewal of hostilities. The soldiers were returning to camp from the fields, when the guards on duty outside the camp gates reported to Caesar that they could see a cloud of dust larger than usual coming toward them from the direction of the returning legion. This confirmed Caesar's suspicions that the barbarians had hatched some new plot. He quickly mobilized his forces and advanced some way out in front of the camp. Soon he could see that the seventh legion was under attack from the enemy and was in difficulties. They had closed ranks, while weapons were raining down on them from all sides.

What had happened was this: as the men had now cut the wheat in all but one of the fields, the enemy were sure that our men would come to that field, and had hidden themselves at night in the woods. Then when our men were scattered over the field and had put down their weapons and were concentrating on cutting the wheat, they

had launched a sudden attack. They had killed a handful of soldiers and thrown the rest into confusion and disarray. At the same moment, the soldiers found themselves surrounded by cavalry and chariots.

This is how the Britons fight from their chariots: first they drive them all over the battlefield, throwing their javelins and inspiring considerable fear in the enemy ranks with their galloping horses and clattering wheels. Then they mingle with the cavalry units, leap down from the chariots, and fight on foot. The charioteers, in the meantime, withdraw a little way from the thick of the fighting and position the chariots so that if the warriors find themselves hard-pressed by enemy numbers, they have a ready means of withdrawing to their own lines. This gives them both the mobility of cavalry and the stability of infantry in battle. As they practice with them every day, they have learned how to keep the horses under control, even when galloping down a steep hill. They can quickly bring them to a halt or make them turn and can even run down the chariot pole and stand on the yoke, and then dash back into the chariot.

STORM DAMAGE

The Romans now learned the truth of the remark that Caesar earlier ascribes to the Veneti— that venturing out into Atlantic waters was something very different from sailing in the comparative safety of the Mediterranean. The storm damage to his ships was a serious threat to Caesar, but as usual he was able to respond to this new emergency quickly and effectively. However, this near disaster and the approach of the autumn equinox (around September 22 or 23), which marked the end of the sailing season, help to account for his hasty return to Gaul.

31

Our men were confused by these unfamiliar tactics, and Caesar came to their rescue just in the nick of time. At his arrival, the enemy came to a standstill, and our forces got over their fright. Despite this success, he did not think it was the right moment for harassing the enemy and provoking a battle. Therefore he maintained his ground and after a short interval led his legions back into camp.

An engagement with the enemy took place soon after this, in which some 30 cavalry took part. These had been supplied to Caesar by Commius, king of the Atrebates. When our men charged, the enemy turned and fled. Our men ran after them as far as they could and killed a considerable number. Then they set fire to all the buildings over a wide area, before returning to camp.

On the same day, envoys sent by the enemy came to Caesar to make peace. Caesar doubled the number of hostages required from them and gave orders for the hostages to be taken over to the Continent, since the autumnal **equinox** was approaching and he did not think his already damaged ships should be exposed to the dangers of a winter crossing. Then when the weather was fine, he set sail. All the ships returned safely to the Continent, but two of the transport ships were unable to reach the same harbor as the others. They were carried a little way down the coast.

This coin was minted in Rome by Lucius Hostilius Saserna within a few years of the start of Caesar's campaigns. It shows a Celtic chariot with its charioteer and mounted warrior, and is now in the Ashmolean Museum in Oxford, England.

Caesar left his winter quarters for Italy, as was his custom each year. He told the officers whom he left in charge of the legions to build as many ships as possible that winter and to have the old ones repaired. He explained exactly how he wanted them built. For speed of loading and to make it easier to beach the ships, he wanted them a little shallower than the ones we regularly use in our own Mediterranean waters, and he wanted them a little wider, to make room for the loads they were to carry, including large numbers of animals. They were all to be fitted with oars as well as sails, and all the material required for their rigging and tackle was ordered from Spain.

When he returned to Gaul from his other duties, he visited all the army's winter quarters. He found that, despite a universal lack of materials of one kind or another, superhuman efforts on the part of his men had succeeded in producing for him 600 or so ships of the kind described, together with 28 warships, and that it was only a matter of a few days before they could be launched. He congratulated the men and the officers who had been in charge of the operation and set out the next stage of his plans. All the ships were to assemble at Portus Itius, for he knew that this was the best departure point on the Continent for a crossing to Britain, which was some 30 miles away. Cavalry from the whole of Gaul also assembled here, numbering 4,000, and together with them came the chiefs of all the tribes. Most of these Caesar had decided to take with him, as hostages, to stop any attempt at an uprising in Gaul during his absence.

For three to four weeks, he was forced to stay in harbor, since northwesterlies, which are the prevailing winds for much of the year in these parts, made sailing impossible. At last, seizing the opportunity of a spell of fine weather, he gave orders for the infantry and cavalry to embark. As dusk was approaching, Caesar set sail, taking with him five legions and 2,000 cavalry.

A light southwesterly wind carried him across the English Channel until about midnight, when the wind dropped and he was unable to continue the crossing. Instead he was carried off course on the tide, and when daylight returned, he saw Britain receding into the distance on his left. Then the tide turned again, and he rowed hard on the incoming tide, in order to reach the part of the island that he knew from the previous summer provided the best landing place. The soldiers deserved high praise for their endurance at this point, for by rowing without stopping, they kept the warships up with the transport ships and other heavy vessels. The whole fleet reached Britain around midday, and not a single enemy soldier was to be seen. Caesar later learned from prisoners that although large forces had assembled there, they had been scared by the vast numbers of

CHAPTER 5

A Little Deeper into Britain

(54 B.C.)

This beautiful bronze shield, now in the British Museum in London, was found in the Thames River. It dates from the first century B.C., and its embossed decoration is set with red glass.

ships, more than 800 in all, and had withdrawn from the coast and hidden on higher ground.

When the troops had been brought ashore and a suitable place found for their camp, Caesar made inquiries among the prisoners and discovered where the enemy forces had taken up position. Leaving some of his army on the shore to protect the ships, he set off in pursuit of the enemy shortly after midnight. He was not unduly worried about the ships, since he had left them anchored on an open, sandy beach. Quintus Atrius was left in charge of keeping them safe.

Soon afterward, Caesar divided his forces and set off again in pursuit of the retreating Britons. However, they were hardly out of sight of the camp when messengers on horseback came to Caesar with news that during the night a violent storm had blown up, and that almost all the ships had been damaged or had run aground. On hearing this, Caesar called a halt and returned to see the damage for himself. About 40 ships had been lost, but it looked as if the remainder could be repaired, with considerable effort. So he picked out all the craftsmen from the legions, and sent for still more to come from the Continent. Meanwhile, despite the immense labor involved, he decided the best thing to do was to haul all the ships ashore and to have them included within the camp fortifications. He spent around ten days building the fortifications, and the soldiers worked day and night to get the task finished.

Caesar left the same forces as before to protect the ships and returned to the place where he had stopped his pursuit of the enemy. Here he found that the Britons had gathered together in greater numbers, and had unanimously given the command to Cassivellaunus. His territory is separated from the coastal tribes by a river called the Thames, some 80 miles inland. In earlier times he and the other tribes had been at constant war with one another, but our arrival had alarmed the Britons, and they had decided to put him in supreme command of the war.

The inland part of Britain is inhabited by people who maintain the tradition that they and their ancestors were born on the island. Those on the coast, on the other hand, are Belgae, who crossed the Channel in search of plunder and to make war and who, when the fighting came to an end, stayed on and started to farm the land. These people mostly keep their earlier tribal names. The population is very large, their buildings are numerous and very like those to be found in Gaul, and they have a great number of cattle. Three different forms of currency are used— bronze, gold coins, and iron bars of a fixed weight. Tin is found inland and iron on the coast, though only in small quantities. The copper that they use is imported. There are all kinds of timber, just as in Gaul, except beech and fir. They do not eat hares, fowl, or geese, but raise these animals just for enjoyment. The climate is milder than in Gaul, with less severe winters.

The island is triangular in shape. One of the three sides faces Gaul, and in one of its corners, to the east, lies Kent. This is where most of the ships from Gaul land. The lower corner faces south, and the whole of this side measures about 500 miles. The second side faces west, toward Spain. In this direction lies Ireland, which is half the size of Britain, so it is thought, and is the same distance from Britain as Britain itself is from Gaul. Halfway across the passage to Ireland lies the Isle of Man. In addition to this, there are thought to be many smaller islands lying off the west coast of Britain. Various writers have claimed that in these islands there is a period of thirty days' total darkness in midwinter. We got no fresh information on this topic, but we did observe, with the aid of measurements by water clock, that the nights were shorter here than on the Continent. The length of the second side is estimated by people here to be 700 miles. The third side of the triangle faces north, with nothing but sea beyond it, except that one of its corners faces more or less toward Germany. Its length is reckoned at 800 miles. So, all the way around, the island measures a distance of 2,000 miles.

By far the most civilized of its inhabitants are those who live in Kent, all of which is a coastal district. Their customs differ little from those of people in Gaul. Farther inland they hardly sow any crops but live instead on milk and meat, and dress in animal skins. All the Britons paint themselves with **woad,** which gives them a dark blue color and makes them all the more terrifying to see in battle. They wear their hair long and shave the rest of their bodies, all except the upper lip. As many as ten or twelve of them have wives in common, and this will generally mean brothers sharing with brothers and fathers with sons. When a baby is born, it is regarded as belonging to the man who first took the mother to bed when she was a girl.

After a number of encounters with the enemy, Caesar led his army to the Thames River, on the borders of Cassivellaunus' territory. There is only one place where this river can be crossed on foot, and that is only with difficulty. He reached this point and saw on

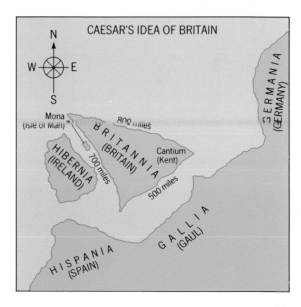

CAESAR'S IDEA OF BRITAIN

THE CELTIC INHABITANTS OF BRITAIN

The **Celtic** civilization of Britain at this time was like that of Gaul, although not as highly developed, except in the southeast, where tribes from Belgic Gaul had recently arrived across the Channel. The Britons still used chariots in war, which were by now out of use in Gaul. Mostly the Britons lived in hut villages or in fortified, upland settlements known as hill forts. Cassivellaunus was king of a tribe called the Catuvellauni, who lived in Middlesex and Hertfordshire. His capital was most probably at Wheathampstead, near St. Albans. The water clock worked on the same principle as the hour glass: water drained at a fixed rate from a raised container into a lower one. In this way you could measure time. When Caesar returned to Gaul, no Roman forces were left behind in Britain. The Romans did not control the country, despite Caesar's claim that he fixed the annual amount of tribute that Britain should pay to Rome.

the opposite bank of the river large forces of the enemy waiting for him. In addition, the bank had been fortified with a line of sharp wooden stakes along its edge, and more of these were hidden under the water. This information came from prisoners and deserters. Caesar sent the cavalry over first and ordered the infantry to follow immediately behind. The soldiers went forward with such speed and determination, despite having only their heads above water, that the enemy could not stand up to the combined onslaught of infantry and cavalry, and abandoned the riverbank and took to their heels.

Cassivellaunus now gave up all hope of fighting a large-scale battle and dismissed the bulk of his forces, keeping only some 4,000 charioteers. With these he harried our advancing forces from hiding places deep in the forests. Eventually Caesar learned from tribes that had surrendered to him where Cassivellaunus' stronghold was. He made straight for it with his legions and found a place with excellent natural defenses and additional fortification. Nevertheless he quickly attacked it on two sides at once. The enemy resistance was brief and soon collapsed under our attack. The Britons fled from another side of the stronghold. A great number of cattle were discovered there, and many of the enemy were either caught or killed as they fled.

While this was going on, Cassivellaunus sent messengers to the four kings who ruled over Kent and told them to join forces and launch a surprise attack on our naval camp. When they reached it, our men burst out of the camp and killed a great number of them, before returning without a single loss. News of this battle reached Cassivellaunus, and coming as it did on top of so many other losses, such devastation to his lands, and a rising threat of rebellion among his peoples, it persuaded him to send envoys to Caesar to surrender. Caesar had decided to be back on the Continent for the winter, for fear of trouble in Gaul, and as only a little of the summer remained now, he demanded hostages and laid down the annual amount of **tribute** that Britain should pay to Rome.

When the hostages arrived, he led his army back to the coast, where he found that the ships had been repaired. Because of the large number of prisoners and the loss of a number of the ships through storm damage, he decided to make the return crossing in two stages. As it turned out, not one troop carrier was lost of all the ships and in the course of all the sailings of this and the previous year.

Gaul as a whole is divided into three parts. In one part live the Belgae, in another the Aquitani, and in the third the Celts (that is their name for themselves, but we call them the Gauls). These three have quite different languages, customs, and laws. The bravest of the three are the Belgae, because they are farthest away from the civilized life and culture of the Roman Province and are hardly ever visited by merchants bringing things that tempt them to relax their warlike energies. Also they are closest to the Germans, who live across the Rhine and with whom they are constantly at war. For the same reason, among the rest of the Gauls it is the Helvetii who stand out for their bravery, since they fight battles virtually every day with the Germans, whenever one side sets foot on the other's territory.

Rival parties exist throughout Gaul at all levels— in every tribe and in every village and local district and even, it could almost be said, within individual households. The leaders of these rival parties are those judged by their followers to have the greatest authority, and decisions of any kind are referred to their judgment. Behind this ancient custom there seems to be the desire to ensure that no

CHAPTER 6

Gaul and Its People

Gaul at the time of Caesar's campaigns.

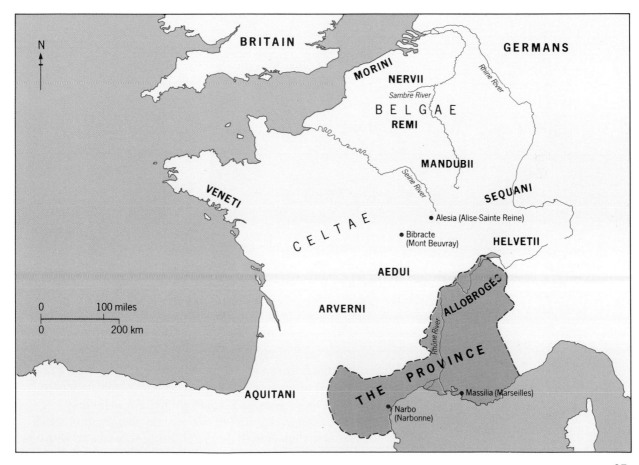

Part of a Celtic sanctuary at Roquepertuse in Provence, southern France. The columns of the temple were carved with niches to hold human heads. The cult of the severed head was widespread among the Celts.

commoner lacks protection against a stronger adversary. No leader will tolerate any violence or trickery against his followers; if he did, he would soon lose his authority. The same system applies on a grand scale within Gaul itself, since all the tribes are divided into two sides.

Throughout the whole of Gaul, there are only two classes that count as having any standing. The common people are hardly better off than slaves. They never dare decide things for themselves, and they are never consulted. Most of them are crushed by debt or by the huge amount of tribute they have to pay, or they are oppressed by those with more power and adopt a life of service to the nobles, who have over them the powers of a master over his slaves. The two classes with authority are the priests, called the **Druids,** and the **knights.**

The Druids take charge of everything to do with religion. They superintend both public and private sacrifices and interpret the will of the gods. A great number of young men flock to them for lessons, and they are held in great respect by all. Almost every dispute, whether public or private, is settled by them. Similarly, if a crime is committed, if someone is murdered, or if there is a dispute over an inheritance or a boundary, they are the ones who make the decision and determine the level of compensation or punishment. If either an individual or a tribe refuses to accept their decision, then they are banned from attending sacrifices. There is no worse punishment in Gaul than this, for those who are banned are treated as godless criminals and are shunned by all. No one will go near them or speak to them for fear that contact with them will bring some awful disaster.

There is a Chief Druid in charge of all the rest, who commands the highest respect. A successor takes over when he dies, and sometimes, if there are rivals, they settle the matter by armed combat. The ideas of the Druids are said to have started in Britain and to have come from there into Gaul. Certainly in our own day, those who want to find out about it generally go to Britain to do so. It is said that pupils studying their teachings have to learn by heart a great number of verses. Some spend as long as twenty years on this. They believe that they must never write their teaching down, although for all kinds of other matters, such as public and private accounts, the Gauls make use of the Greek alphabet.

The most important belief that the Druids wish people to adopt is that the soul does not die, but passes after death from one body to another. This, they believe, helps people to be brave, since it takes away the fear of death. Besides this, they discuss at great length the stars and their movements, the size of the universe and of the earth, the way the world is made up, and the power and influence of the immortal gods. Their teachings on all these matters they pass on to the young.

The other class is that of the knights. When they are needed in war (and before Caesar's arrival this happened almost every year), they all take part in the fighting. The ones that come from the greatest families and have the most wealth surround themselves with the largest number of men. The Gauls mark the outbreak of war by calling an assembly of armed warriors. It is the law throughout their land that all adult warriors should heed this call. He who is the last to arrive suffers every kind of torture before being put to death in the sight of the whole army.

The Gauls are a most superstitious nation. They practice human sacrifice with the aid of their Druids, as they believe that the goodwill of the gods cannot be won without shedding human blood. In some cases they construct images of a colossal size, whose limbs are plaited together out of wickerwork and filled with living people. They are then set on fire, and as the flames surround them, the people are burned to death. In their view the gods prefer it when those who are put to death in this way are convicted thieves, robbers, and other guilty people, but when the supply of these runs out, they will even descend to putting innocent people to death.

The god they hold in most respect is Mercury, making most images of him, and regarding him as the inventor of all arts, the guide on all men's paths and journeys, and the patron-in-chief of money-making and merchandise. Next to him they worship Apollo, Mars, Jupiter, and Minerva, holding more or less the same beliefs about them as

THE INHABITANTS OF GAUL

The people of Gaul in Caesar's time did not form what we would describe as a nation. Gaul was made up of many tribes at different stages of social development, so that Caesar's description of their way of life is only a generalized one. Gallic society seems to have resembled the feudal system found later in the Middle Ages. Noble families, whom Caesar calls the "knights," provided protection to the poorer freemen farmers. The farmers and their slaves worked the land and owed their allegiance to a particular nobleman. The Druids were the priests, who kept the Gauls in touch with their gods and goddesses and handed down traditional learning and skills.

other peoples do (such as that Apollo cures disease, Minerva passes on the principles of industry and handicrafts, Jupiter holds sway over the gods, and Mars rules over war). Most of the **spoils** taken in war are dedicated to Mars, and among many of the tribes, vast mounds of these spoils can be seen from far and wide in holy places. Hardly anyone will dare to hide his own part of these spoils at home, or take anything from the pile, knowing that his religion decrees a hideous death under torture for such action.

Every one of the Gauls claims he is descended from Father Dis. This tradition, they say, is handed down by the Druids. For this reason, they measure the passage of time not in days but in nights. When a man marries, he matches from his own pocket the amount brought to him by his wife's **dowry**. The whole amount is then kept in one single account, and any profit made is set aside. Then whichever partner outlives the other gets both halves of the money, together with the profits that have accumulated over the years. A man has the power of life and death over his wife and his children. If the head of an important family dies in suspicious circumstances, his relatives will question his widow, just as though she were a slave. If found guilty, she is tortured in every way imaginable and then burned alive. Considering the level of civilization the Gauls have reached, their funerals are both magnificent and lavish. Whatever was thought to be dear to the departed during his lifetime goes into the flames. This includes animals, and not so very long ago, slaves and faithful **retainers.** When the funeral rites were duly performed, they, too, were burned with their master.

When all his cavalry had been put to flight, Vercingetorix withdrew to Alesia. Caesar pursued him for the remaining hours of daylight and killed some 3,000 of the enemy rear guard. The next day he pitched camp close to Alesia. This fortified town stood in a commanding position at the top of a high hill. The only way to take it appeared to be by **blockade.** Two rivers ran at the foot of the hill, one on the north side and the other on the south. A plain lay in front of Alesia, stretching out for some 3 miles, and in the middle distance, a ring of high hills surrounded the town on all its remaining sides. The whole eastern side of the hill, below the defensive wall of the stronghold, was filled with Gallic forces, who had made a ditch and a 6-foot-high wall around their position. The siege works now being undertaken by the Romans ran for a total of 11 miles around the whole area. Camps enjoying good vantage points were constructed, and 23 watchtowers were manned day and night, in case of a surprise counterattack.

When the work of blockading the town had begun, a fierce cavalry battle took place on the plain in front of the town. German auxiliaries fighting on the Roman side helped to produce a great slaughter of the Gallic forces. Vercingetorix then decided to send all his cavalry forces away by night, before the siege works were completed by the Romans. As they left, he gave them orders to return home to their own tribes and to call up all those who were able to bear arms. He had, he said, enough wheat within the town to last with care for about a month. He then ordered all the wheat to be brought to him. Anyone found disobeying this order was executed. There was plenty of livestock, and this he distributed among his men. The wheat he arranged to be measured out to everyone, a little at a time, and all the forces that had originally been stationed in front of the town were now brought inside. Having made these arrangements, he prepared to carry on the war and to wait for help to arrive from Gaul.

Caesar learned all this from deserters and prisoners and arranged for more extensive siege works to be built. Deep trenches were dug, more walls and turrets built, and a second, outer line of earthworks constructed to protect the forces besieging the town. Pits were made and filled with vertical wooden stakes sharpened to a point and hidden just below the level of the ground, so that anyone who trod on them would be impaled. Strewn all around in front of these pits were blocks of wood hammered into the ground, with iron hooks projecting from them.

While all this was happening at Alesia, the Gauls summoned a council of war. About 8,000 cavalry and 250,000 infantry were assembled. One of the commanders-in-chief of this army was

CHAPTER 7

Last Stand

(52 B.C.)

THE REBELLION OF VERCINGETORIX

The most serious rebellion Caesar had to deal with during his years in Gaul was that of Vercingetorix, leader of the Arvernian tribe, in 52 B.C. Vercingetorix tried to develop a sense of **nationalism** among the Gallic tribes, in the face of permanent occupation by the Romans. The rebellion spread quickly. Caesar's former ally, Commius, king of the Atrebates, became one of its ringleaders. Vercingetorix posed more problems for Caesar and his forces than any other Gallic commander. He adopted a "scorched earth" policy in his war with the Romans, whereby anything that might have been useful to the enemy was burned or removed. Eventually, Vercingetorix was forced to make a last stand in the hill town of Alesia (Alise-Sainte-Reine on Mount Auxois in present-day France).

Commius, the Atrebatian. In earlier years, Caesar had made use of this man Commius in Britain, regarding him as a loyal and valuable friend, and rewarding him and his people for their services. Now, however, there was such a universal desire in Gaul to win back their freedom and recover their former glory in war that no memory of favors or friendship was allowed to stand in its way. All were united in their efforts to prepare for war. The whole force set out for Alesia full of enthusiasm and confidence. Each man said to himself that the sight alone of such a vast army would be enough to unnerve the enemy, especially since they would then have to fight on two fronts, for the defenders would launch an attack the moment they saw the huge numbers of cavalry and infantry coming to relieve them.

The siege of Alesia continued. The day on which they had been expecting their relief forces to arrive passed. All their wheat had now been used up, and they had no idea what was being done to help them. They called a meeting to discuss what was to become of them. All kinds of suggestions were made, including one in particular that showed incredible wickedness and cruelty. This was that rather than surrender, they should keep alive by eating the flesh of those who could not fight. When all the suggestions had been heard, it was decided to remove from the town all those who for any reason were unable to fight, and only to make use of this last proposal if all else failed. The Mandubii, who had received Vercingetorix's forces into their town, were told to leave with their families. They now came to the Roman fortifications and, crying aloud and weeping, begged to be given food and

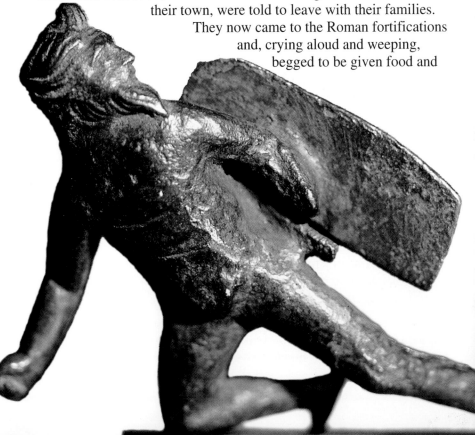

Statue of a falling Gallic warrior.

become Roman slaves, but the guards on duty had orders from Caesar to turn them away.

Commius and the other commanders-in-chief, meanwhile, arrived outside Alesia with all their forces and took up position on a hill not more than a mile away from our lines of fortification. The next day the cavalry was brought out of camp and filled the whole plain in front of the town. The infantry forces were withdrawn a little way and took up position on higher ground. The town of Alesia commanded a fine view of the plain below. When the people in the town saw that help had arrived, they crowded together to congratulate each other on their escape. Everyone was in high spirits. They brought their forces out in front of the town, filled the first trench, and made ready for an attack.

Caesar placed all his infantry along his two lines of fortification, one facing the town, the other facing the Gallic relief forces. Then he ordered the cavalry out into battle. All the camps on the surrounding high ground had a clear view of the plain below, and every soldier watched intently to see how the battle would end. The Gauls under siege in Alesia and those who had come to their aid shouted and screamed on all sides to urge their men on. Because the two sides knew that all eyes were fixed on them and that no act of bravery or of cowardice would go unnoticed, the desire to gain glory and the dread of being branded a coward drove both sides on to greater deeds of valor. The battle raged from midday almost until sunset, with victory hanging in the balance. Then the German cavalry made one massive drive against the enemy and pushed them back. The archers who had been giving the Gauls covering fire were surrounded and killed. Our men then pursued the retreating forces on all sides relentlessly, as far as their camp. Those who had come out of Alesia went sadly back into the town. Victory had eluded them.

One day went by, and the Gauls made another attempt on our position. At dead of night, the relieving forces moved silently out of camp with large bundles of brushwood, ladders, and **grappling hooks** in their hands. Suddenly they gave a great shout to let the forces in Alesia know that they were coming. They threw the brushwood into the trenches but met with a hail of missiles from our men. At the same time, hearing the shout, Vercingetorix sounded the call to arms and led his forces out of the town. No one could see what was happening in the dark, and the casualties on both sides were high. While they remained

THE SIEGE OF ALESIA

The Roman army had plenty of experience of laying siege to enemy towns. They dug out camps for themselves every day while they were on the move and were used to earthworks. However, the siege of Alesia was on a gigantic scale. The circle of fortification around Alesia was 11 miles long. This was then surrounded by outer lines to protect the Romans from the large Gallic army that came to relieve the town. In the 1860s, French archaeologists excavated the site of Caesar's siegeworks around Alesia. More recently aerial photography, using infrared techniques, has shown the evidence of Roman military works.

some distance away from our fortifications, the Gauls had the upper hand with the greater volume of their missiles. But when they got nearer, they found to their surprise that they were caught on the iron hooks or pitched into the hidden traps and impaled on the sharpened stakes. Others fell victim to the javelins launched by our heavy catapults from the walls. Their wounds were numerous, and when daylight returned, at no point had our defenses been breached.

The relieving forces were afraid now of being outflanked by our soldiers who were camped on the higher ground and withdrew to their own lines. It had taken time for Vercingetorix and his men to bring all their equipment out of Alesia and to fill the first trenches. They had still not reached our fortifications when they heard that their allies had withdrawn, and then they returned to the town, with nothing accomplished.

The Gauls had twice now been driven back with great losses. They held a council to decide on their next move and discovered from people who knew the locality that there was a hill to the north which, because it extended so far, our men had not been able to include within the blockade of the town. They had no choice here but to pitch camp on slightly unfavorable, sloping ground. The enemy commanders sent a reconnaissance party to make sure of the position and then selected 60,000 warriors from those tribes that had the highest reputation for bravery. These set out from camp as night fell, hid under cover of the hill, and by a prearranged plan advanced on the Roman camp as midday was approaching. Simultaneously, the Gallic cavalry moved in on our fortifications in the plain, and the remaining forces made a show of strength in front of their own camp.

Vercingetorix saw all this happen from the citadel of Alesia and led his forces out of the town. He brought out bundles of brushwood, poles, protective sheds, grappling hooks, and anything else that could help them launch their attack. There was fighting going on everywhere at once, and every device was tried. Charges were made on what appeared to be our weakest points, and the Roman forces were stretched to their limit.

Caesar had found a good position from which to see what was happening all over the battlefield and to send help where it was most needed. Both sides knew that they must put all their energies into this struggle. Weapons on our side were running short; the men were almost at the breaking point. Caesar first sent reinforcements, then hastened into the fighting himself. The special color of his cloak showed everyone that he had arrived. Cavalry and infantry brigades that had orders to follow him were now clearly visible coming down from the higher ground. Our men had passed now from using spears

RESISTANCE TO THE ROMANS COLLAPSES

Although fighting continued for another two years, the fall of Alesia marked the end of Gallic resistance to Roman occupation. The Romans had been in Gaul now for seven years, and after so many losses, there was neither the will nor the ability to mount widespread resistance. Caesar's narrative of the Gallic War ends at this point.

to fighting with their swords. Suddenly our cavalry could be seen behind the enemy, and fresh forces were coming toward them from the front. The enemy turned and fled. There was a great slaughter. Few of their vast forces got safely back to camp. Those in Alesia saw the slaughter and the flight of their countrymen. They gave up all hope and brought their forces back from our fortifications. The moment news of this reached the Gauls' camp, they all ran away. The cavalry was sent after them around midnight and caught up with those at the back of the column. A large number were either captured or killed. The rest fled until they had dispersed to their own tribes.

The next day envoys were sent to Caesar from Alesia. He ordered them to lay down their arms and send their chieftains to him. He himself took up a seat on the fortifications in front of the camp. The leaders were sent to him there. Vercingetorix was handed over and all their weapons were thrown down. Almost all the prisoners were given as a reward to the whole army, one to each soldier. He now sent the legions to their various winter quarters, having decided to spend the winter himself in Bibracte. When this news reached Rome, twenty days were given over to a public thanksgiving.

A silver cup from Boscoreale, showing a scene from a triumphal Roman procession. Conquering generals returning in triumph to Rome put on lavish processions to show off to the Roman people the treasures and the prisoners they had captured. Vercingetorix was paraded in such a procession by Caesar, before being executed.

Glossary

auxiliary forces additional soldiers, over and above the regular infantrymen, that made up the legions. Caesar's auxiliary forces included cavalry, archers, slingers, and light infantry. These forces served on a less permanent basis than the legionary soldiers.

barbarians people who lived outside the Roman Empire, who did not speak Greek or Latin. The Romans thought the barbarians uncivilized and fit only for slavery.

blockade surrounding of a place by an enemy to prevent entry and exit.

booty/spoils the prizes of war taken from the enemy on the battlefield.

Celtic/Celts the general term for the inhabitants at this time of the lands north of the Mediterranean region, broadly sharing a common language and traditions.

centurion an experienced legionary soldier in command of 80-100 men. The centurions played a key role in Caesar's army.

consuls the two most senior officials in the Roman government. They were elected to serve for one year and combined political and military command. Years were dated by reference to the names of the two consuls.

delegation/envoys a party of people sent on an official mission, often to speak with an enemy commander.

dowry a sum of money or articles of value brought by a bride to give to her husband at their wedding.

Druids term used by Caesar for the priests of Celtic Gaul and Britain.

equinox twice in the year, once about March 21 and the other about September 22 or 23, when day and night are of equal length. The autumnal equinox marked the end of the sailing season for the Romans.

flax the plant from which canvas for sails was made.

grappling hooks/grappling irons claw-like hooks made of iron and mounted on poles for seizing hold of enemy walls.

Helvetii a Celtic tribe living in present-day western Switzerland.

knights the noble families among the Gauls, who were rich enough to keep horses for use in battle. They should not be thought of as the knights in armor, found later in the Middle Ages, although the society in which they lived resembled the feudalism of the Middle Ages in some ways.

legion the regular unit of the Roman army, numbering some 5,000 infantry soldiers. The legionary soldiers were armed with a throwing spear, a sword, and a dagger, and were a highly efficient fighting force.

marines seaborne soldiers.

military tribunes young officers of well-to-do families, serving a term as military commanders before going on to careers in public service.

nationalism   the sense of belonging to one nation, sharing a common language and institutions, and valuing its independence.

officers of Caesar   officers to whom Caesar owed much of his success and who worked under him, but about whom he says comparatively little.

Province   an area formed in the deep south of France and controlled by the Romans. The countries around the Mediterranean were coming under Roman control at this time. Once conquered, they became Roman provinces and were ruled by the Romans.

quaestor   officer in the army, whose main task was financial but who on occasions was given command of forces.

retainers   people attached to high-ranking families in a position of service.

sarcophagus   decorated stone or marble coffin.

shoals   shallow water; often concealing dangerous sand banks.

standards   decorated poles raised to show the rallying points for the soldiers. A special form of standard was the legionary eagle, carried into battle by the eagle-bearer.

torc   a necklace of twisted metal.

tribute   tax payable by one group of people to another who had control over them. People in the Roman provinces had to pay tribute to the Roman state.

woad   a dark blue vegetable dye, used by the Britons for decorating themselves.

yardarm   the arm attached near the top of a mast, from which the sail hung.

Index

Numbers in *italic* type refer to captions; numbers in **bold** type refer to information boxes.

Selection, translation, and additional material
© Heinemann Educational 1993